It's not Crazy,
It's Genius!

HEATHER GIFFORD

DEDICATION

For my darling boys,
Tom and Mathew.

Live life to the full.
Love deeply and intensely.
Keep laughing at this crazy, mysterious and wonderful
life.

Always and Forever.
Love.

CONTENTS

ACKNOWLEDGEMENTS

I would like to thank all my clients, past and present, for giving me the opportunity to learn, grow and share my creativity and craziness! I am forever grateful.

"Here's to the crazy ones, the misfits, the rebels, the troublemakers, the round pegs in the square holes... the ones who see things differently -- they're not fond of rules... You can quote them, disagree with them, glorify or vilify them, but the only thing you can't do is ignore them because they change things... they push the human race forward, and while some may see them as the crazy ones, we see genius, because the ones who are crazy enough to think that they can change the world, are the ones who do."

~ Steve Jobs – US Computer Engineer & Industrialist (1955-2011)

The accountant looked on in disbelief as his mouth dropped open, "What do you mean he has to stand on his head?" his eyes widened.   The client, on the other hand, puzzled and intrigued by my statement, leant forward in his chair, "Go on..." he said.

CRAZY BUSINESS TIP # 1

Stand on your head ... or become a Salmon, it's entirely up to you!

In business, it's so easy to keep going in the same direction and hope for a different result.   It rarely works, trust me on this.

In the famous quote (which most attribute to Albert Einstein, but was first mentioned in a book by author Rita Mae Brown) it is said that the definition of insanity is doing the same thing over and over again but expecting different results. I agree.

You have a choice – you can be mainstream and enjoy a reasonable, but constantly challenging existence. Or, you can be different and stand out from the mediocre business crowd. Make a difference and BE the difference.

The best way I've seen of achieving this in business is... to stand on your head!

Not literally you understand, although I should mention that it does have very powerful health benefits if you can manage to do it from time to time.

You see, we don't often have the opportunity to view the world from this angle and by doing so, it can bring about a wide variety of amazing benefits to you and your business.

The first thing to do is look at what everyone else in your business sector is doing and then do the exact opposite!

I'm going to give you another analogy, if you can cope with it ...

Imagine everyone in a certain business sector is a fish and they're all swimming in the same direction, they're all fighting for the same food, same space, same attention.

I want you to think Salmon! If you can swim against the other fish, upstream (and by the way, that takes courage, determination and strength) you will automatically stand out from the crowd and in a 'crowded market place' this will give you a strong differential.

By example: A photographer.

 He had followed the crowd by launching his business the same old, same old - photographing children and weddings – and nearly went broke because of it.   Believe me, if you want mediocrity in business, follow the crowd and do what everyone else is doing.

By getting him to 'stand on his head' or swim against the fish, I got him to look at the gaps in the market and the other end of the photography spectrum. I asked him to focus on the difference and his unique passion.

Whilst many of his peer group are focusing on the mainstream weddings and young children market (and struggling to make a living during the economic downturn), I got him to look at the over 50s market (more disposal income, children graduating and leaving home, thus leaving a big emotional gap) and of course, the grandparent and grandchildren market.

As a portrait photographer, he now works specifically with people who value the art of traditional photography, they're more willing to pay for it because of the quality, living history and heritage it provides for future generations.

The majority of his peer group are still focusing on the 'throw-away' society who use their mobile phone to take photographs and readily snap pictures every hour to add to their Facebook profiles.

It is little wonder that they show no interest or respect for professional photographers because they think they can do it themselves.

"No, I won't help you do that." I looked straight into her eyes. "Oh," she said abruptly, she was obviously not used to a consultant refusing to work with her. With an utter look of disbelief on her face, she asked me why not? "Because it's not your true passion. It's not where your heart is and I believe you should be making a difference to the world in another way... I'll help you do that."

CRAZY BUSINESS TIP #2

Listen to your heart, it's calling for you *(sorry that was very nearly a Roxette moment!).*

You'll always get, what you've always done.

Nothing kills business inspiration and making a difference to the lives of others, than staying in your comfort zone.

The amount of business people who I've met over the years that are 'dead behind the eyes' are too many to count, sadly.

I think they were excited at one point in their lives, perhaps when they first entered self-employment?

They probably woke up one day and declared, "That's it, I can do my boss's job better than they can, so I'm going to set up my own business!" Yeah, that's usually the way the majority enter self-employment.

People crave the freedom of being their own boss, and then realise they've just swapped their day job for less pay, less security and less annual leave. Ho hum!

And, I'm no different. I didn't wake up sixteen years ago and declare "I'm going to change the world!". I entered self-employment and stuck to what I knew best and my past experience, and it's an excellent place to start.

Did I enjoy it? Yes I suppose I did. Did it help others? Yes, it boosted their egos and the bank balances. Did I feel my true calling? Categorically, with a one word answer - NO.

We all enter self employment at different stages in our personal development and life. You may have had many years of experience that you can now tap into and you're fully aware of your gifts, talents and passion.

I was 27 when I first became self-employed. I knew my craft well enough to make a decent living, I was enthusiastic for creating my own business ... but I hadn't yet discovered my individuality and personal passion. My head ruled my business (and at the time, my personal life) and my heart didn't get a look in!

I've got to say honestly that it took many, many years for me to truly have the courage to step into my own individuality and step away from the safe 'expected' route.

But when I did, I found greater fulfillment, wealth and service to others.

The question I'd like you to ask yourself is what fuels you? What is your passion? What do you do naturally each day, without being paid for doing it?

This is when you'll start to discover your very own recipe for success and happiness. It's your USP, and what I believe that stands for is your *'Unique Saleable Passion™'*.

By example: A business coach.

She was very good and competent as a business coach and she did it because she'd always done it. But when I looked into her eyes as she talked, the 'light' wasn't on.

On a personal level, her young son has Autism; she knows what it's like to raise a child with these challenges and the effect it has on a family unit.

When I asked her what she really wanted to do before she died, she told me how she wanted to support and change the lives of thousands of families who have to cope alone, every day with Autism.   Now, that's a true passion, if ever there was.

I declined helping her with the business coaching, but said I'd move mountains to help her achieve her passion and goal.

We worked together and I helped her formulate and launch her first website, the seedling of an idea, made real.

I'm delighted to say that she now runs a registered UK-wide charity that helps, supports and assists families with Autism.

When you're passionate about something, you can achieve anything. It's a very powerful driving force and motivator.

So, what's your **Unique Saleable Passion™**?

"It's too difficult, I can't do it," tears welled up in her eyes, and in that moment I understood her pain. I gently put my hand on hers, "I want you to tell your story to inspire others. I know this will be difficult for you, but if it wasn't - everyone would be doing it."

CRAZY BUSINESS TIP #3

Dig deep, your pain is your greatest gift.

I've always believed that in life things happen for a reason.

Often, it's the people who have experienced the greatest hardship and pain who make the biggest difference to others.

Empathy is all about emotional capacity. It is about being able to put yourself in the 'emotional place' of others.

The truest form of empathy, and the most powerful one for making a difference in the world is when you can tap into your own experiences, dig deep and have the courage to share and help others.

What experience in your life has caused you pain? How could you support others by sharing your personal story of how you overcame your particular life challenge?

Why not use it as a 'platform' to help and serve others. You don't need to stay in the past with the hurt and pain, simply channel it, learn from it, and then lever the experience to help other people who think they don't have a choice.

By example: A life coach.

She was playing it safe, until she met me.

We talked and she explained that she wanted to help and inspire others who felt they couldn't get themselves out of a 'rut'.

At first she stuck to the same conversation that I've heard a thousand times from coaches – I want to help others.

That's very admirable and a life in service is excellent and fulfilling. It can also leave you totally broke if you don't find a niche and a specialist area – especially in the coaching industry.

I believe it was about an hour into the conversation, when we stopped talking about her coaching and she finally started telling me 'her story'.

We all have stories that we tell ourselves and others – sometimes these can trap us in the past, or liberate us to move forward.

She told me how she had spiraled into depression and lost almost everything that had mattered to her.

A background in corporate, high pressure and demanding, had affected her health, she lost her home and then her relationship failed – within a very short space of time.

One Christmas, she found herself standing in the snow, in her slippers and wondering how life could have got so bad.

From the ashes, just like a phoenix, she managed to rebuild her life.   But she found it difficult to talk about her personal journey and throughout the conversation with me, she cried.

Yeah, I have this knack of dissolving some of my clients to tears … but I've got to say, when that happens, I know I've got a person in front of me who has a very powerful story to share with the world.

Through gentle and sometimes not so gentle mentoring, I supported her to write and publish her first book about her personal journey through depression and out the other side.

She now coaches and speaks at an international level, inspiring others to move forward in their life and overcome adversity through sharing the tools and techniques that have helped her to change and improve her life.

PS. We can now have a full conversation about 'her story' and instead of tears, there are plenty of smiles.

He took a deep breath and swallowed hard: "I was a lorry driver. I had a serious accident and the man who saved my life was profoundly deaf. I never had the opportunity to thank him personally for saving my life, so I decided to dedicate the remainder of my life to helping the deaf community."

For once (and it doesn't happen very often) I was completely speechless.

CRAZY BUSINESS TIP #4

it's about finding the right people, at the right time.

Synchronicity is where it's at baby! The people, the locations, the reasons, the *'why's'* are all taken care of as far as I'm concerned.

When you meet someone, there is ALWAYS a reason ... and in business and life it's all about keeping your eyes and ears open and taking notice.

I like the *Magic of Connection™* approach when it comes to growing a business and that you're either the teacher or the student ... and by the way, that's not always obvious which one you are at the time, sometimes you're both.

If you find clarity in what you want and what you can offer others, people will be drawn to you like iron filings to a magnet!

You'll find each other, at the right time, at the right place.

For me and this gentleman (total strangers) it happened to be an ice-skating rink, of all places.

I don't enjoy ice-skating very much, due to me falling over and getting concussed when I was in my early twenties, so when my children suggested going to the ice-rink that day, I groaned in my usual manner and protested, but they were very persistent and so we went.

As my two sons confidently spun around the ice, I sipped on my coffee and tried to keep my hands warm. It was a couple of days before Christmas.

Mathew then came off the ice momentarily for me to secure his ice-skates. He was also pestering me for more food and drink – just as growing lads do!

I told him to get back on the ice and "I'll see", which basically in parent talk means "I hope you'll forget about that request!".

As I sent him back onto the ice, I let out a sigh indicating a mix of frustration and boredom, which didn't go un-noticed by a kind looking gentleman who had appeared nearby.

"Kid's huh?" he said with a smile. I looked up and acknowledged him with a shrug and a smile.

I don't usually talk to strangers. I believe it stems from my overly protective mother stating quite firmly, over and over again, "Don't talk to strangers!" and implying that 'they' were all mad, axe murderers! Anyway, I digress.

He decided to carry on talking. Not wanting to appear rude, but I would have just left it at the shrug and the smile.

"I'm here with my kids, well... they're not actually my kids," he said, shifting uncomfortably at the confusion that his comment may have caused.

I smiled and looked sideways at him, joking, "What? Have you stolen them?!"

We both laughed and he explained that he worked for the deaf community. He had brought some of the children ice-skating, as a treat.

I immediately relaxed in his presence and we carried on chatting.

Not only did he have an inspiring story to tell, which left me in awe of him, but it turned out that I could help him.

He wanted to bring a product to market which could potentially enhance the lives of thousands of people around the planet.

By example: A translator for the deaf community.

He had dedicated his life to helping the deaf community, by learning sign language, after a near death experience.

When his grandmother had a stroke he felt frustrated and angry at the loss of her dignity because she couldn't get people to understand what she needed/wanted.

The paralysis on one side of her body meant that it was difficult to teach her any of the traditional sign language that use both hands.

 So, he innovated.   He took the two handed sign-language and simplified it to a new single-handed sign system, specifically to aid those who have lost speech and the use of one side of their body – stroke sufferers, head injury patients etc.

For three years he worked on the idea and although everyone he talked to in the medical profession and families who had experienced the frustration of not being able to communicate with a loved one, said it was a great idea, he couldn't find anyone to help him make the dream a reality.

A 'chance' meeting at an ice-skating rink changed all that.

I listened carefully to his idea that day, and without hesitation I said, "Well for a start we need to make it a reality – you need a product, I can help you with that if you want me to."

Together, we have produced the product, packaged it and we're in the process of promoting it worldwide to help thousands of people – now that's the beauty of the Law of Attraction and synchronicity made real!

Time and place people, time and place.

PS. Remember, gifts can come in all kinds of packages!

"But It's been the name of my family business for over 100 years and they're telling me I can't trade under it for legal reasons?," she said softly as the colour drained from her face. I placed my hand gently on her arm and whispered "We'll find a way ... there's always a way."

CRAZY BUSINESS TIP #5

Think of major change as a huge opportunity, not as a threat.

OK, so easier said than done, I realise that. When you're in it, it's not easy to be fully objective and unemotional.

Change can be difficult in life and business, simply because it takes us out of our comfort zone. If you've built systems that are rock solid and cemented certain behaviors in place, then over time, you probably get too relaxed and complacent.

Complacency is dangerous. When we stick to the 'same old, same old' and go through the motions each day, we could be overlooking an important aspect that won't come to light until a big problem occurs.

In this instance, it was a trademark legality which signaled a huge change for my client and the biggest opportunity for growth. It also meant them letting go of the past and looking to the future.

So, crazy tip #5 has two parts:

(1) Make sure your trading name is trademarked and protected, to avoid any costly legal fight for your right to trade under an established business name.   It is a complex area and there are loop holes that won't automatically protect you and your business.

(2) Sometimes, walking away is the best choice. Because with it brings growth and opportunity. Throwing off those shackles = FREEDOM!

By example: A food manufacturer:

For more than a century the business had been run in a certain way, with a certain name and a particular product.

It was quite a complex business situation, as this was a multi-generational business, with several family members running different businesses, independently of each other – but using the same family recipe, product and family trading name.

Everything was going wonderfully, until two of the families disagreed on something. They were located in the same town and when the relationship broke down irretrievably, so did the business model.

All of a sudden, it wasn't easy anymore to keep trading under the same name, with the same type of product in the same way.   To complicate matters, a joint trademark (that previously had protected my client) had lapsed and the other family had applied for a new one, several years previous, in their own names.

This was fine and went unnoticed when relationships were working well. However, when things went wrong, an automatic claim on the name and trademark became the legal right of the other family members.

Trademark law 'trumps' any other means of business trading protection in the UK. This meant my client faced legal action from members of their own family.

Yes, they could have fought this in the courts with a long, drawn out battle and paid a hefty price in terms of legal fees and distraction from running a business. Instead, they took the boldest and most courageous decision – they walked away!

Now, some of you may not understand this decision. You may question WHY they would part with a recognized trading name and brand.

All I can say is nothing is ever as simple as it may appear to an outsider. The choice was made because after careful consideration of all the options available, it made the best commercial, financial and personal sense to walk away and rebrand.

This company had to stop and change the way it did things, but by doing this, it injected new opportunities and opened more doors for trading.

Previously, because of local family trading constraints it hadn't bothered to look at national and international sales opportunities.

With a new trading name came freedom from the old and opportunities from the new.

We changed the name, changed the brand, innovated the product range and entered new markets.   All with a heritage of experience and expertise behind it.

The company is now growing without the restrictions that held its growth back for many years.

The most liberating thing is that it doesn't have to keep looking in the rear view mirror!

Please remember that the past is powerful, but the future is yours for the creating.

"Just when the caterpillar thought the world was over ... It became a beautiful butterfly."

"Do you want to hear something crazy?" she said, slurping at her tea as she continued, "I want to train to become a presenter on stage and do loads of talks." I looked blankly at her, smiled and said nonchalantly, "That's not crazy – today I've been ordained as a Spiritual Minister ... now that's CRAZY!"

CRAZY BUSINESS TIP #6

Stretching your comfort zone isn't crazy; it can be fun, if you let it!

What did you do today that stretched you? I don't mean going to the gym, by the way.

What took you out of your everyday comfort zone?

What did you learn today?

True growth is when we stretch ourselves and the more you stretch, the stronger you become – as anyone who does yoga on a regular basis will testify.

For some, that's standing up for the first time and speaking to an audience. For others, it is jumping out of an airplane.

For me ... oh, let's not go there. I'm one crazy chick.

Apart from making myself feel slightly uncomfortable each day by doing something new, or learning something new, or challenging my beliefs and ideas about something or someone, I try to do ONE major new thing every year.

I choose something that sparks my interest, stretches me and is different from the normal (yeah, that's harder than you imagine where I'm concerned!).

The beauty about this practice is that you grow as a person through experiences and meeting new people – and that's great for you and your business, and your customers.

Remember, if you're bored, it just means you're being boring! *blows raspberry!*

By example: How crazy can you be?

I'd like you do a personal experiment into understanding what you'd really love to do with the rest of your life!

Write down 100 things that you want to do before you die/expire/cease-to-be/move on/pass over/kick the bucket....croak it!

This is fairly challenging, however, stick at it and write down all the crazy little things (and big things) that you want to do in your life – then start ticking them off your list!

You'll be amazed at the vitality and energy this will bring to your life and other people you come into contact with.

It will also make you feel ALIVE! This is great because it raises your vibration level to the enthusiasm, excitement, passion, joy, gratitude and love.   Most of the population, by the way, live below this line in desperate boredom, despair, disappointment and worry.

So, kick off your heels (yes, if you're a man please take them off!) and get busy on injecting some life back into living.

PS. If anyone tells you that having a tattoo on your bum doesn't hurt – they're lying! It does... A LOT!

"I need a local distribution channel," I said firmly. "Like what?" he said, glancing up from his cornflakes. "I need to set up some florists shops... now, how do I become a florist?"

CRAZY BUSINESS TIP #7

Do what you need to do, in order to make it happen!

We all work differently in business. Some of us first need clarity of what we want; some of us need a business structure and some of us just go ahead and do it and then run around like 'headless chickens' because we don't have the clarity or the structure in place!

My personal recipe of success, when it comes to creating any business, lies with the CLARITY: STUCTURE: ACTION route.

I first get very clear about what I want, I then look at different business models (tweaking here and there to fit my own needs and desires) and then I DO IT!

This also works really well with how I coach my clients, I follow the same formula and can work really quickly – well, as fast as my clients can go.

I wanted to share a story of how I used my 'recipe of business success' to enter an industry where I had NO EXPERIENCE at all.

I was one of those women who naturally recoiled at the mention of flower arranging workshops (apologies to any WI members reading this) and I certainly couldn't even put flowers in a vase properly, so even I swallowed hard at the thought of opening a chain of florists.

There was personal and business motivation for this decision. At the time, I owned a manufacturing company that specialized in gift hampers.

One of my biggest headaches with this business was getting my products distributed on a national basis – mainly because they were extremely fragile and the customer wasn't willing to pay for the high postage and packaging costs.

Floristry was a good fit as it had a local distribution base and the same demographic as my existing business (female aged 30-65).

I got clear on my intention to create a contemporary style florist that I could replicate across the UK. I wanted to enter the market hard and fast, in the same city, in two different locations – that way I would block any potential competition and be a serious player.

I also have a rule in business that I never get someone to do what I haven't done myself – so I needed to get experience of floristry, even though I had full intention of employing a team of fully qualified florists.

I pushed aside my fear of incompetence where flower arranging was concerned and enrolled on a two week intensive Interflora course for professionals.

Let me continue the story by sharing how fast you can do something when you have CLARITY: STRUCTURE and take ACTION.

By example: The incompetent flower arranger turned Florist!

I got very clear on what I wanted to do. Open two florists simultaneously with a new 'high end' concept that would act as a local distribution/manufacturing base for my gift hamper business.

I searched online and found a two week intensive Interflora course and learnt how to create flower arrangements and hand-tied bouquets. That gave me real insight into the practical side of the business.

I bought and rebranded one existing florist and then set up a new florist from scratch at another location.

In just six months I'd sourced premises, created a brand, built a website and created marketing materials, overseen a complete store refit, employed two teams of employees, set up systems and sourced suppliers – for not one, but two businesses!

Now, before you shake your head and say "Oh, well that's you." All you need to discover is your 'business success formula'.

When you discover this, you'll have gained the greatest insight into how FAST, SMOOTH and EFFECTIVELY you can make things happen.

PS. What did I learn most about setting up this type of business? I learnt to do more extensive research into buying patterns, because as I discovered after opening, one of the busiest trading times is actually Christmas, which clashed completely with gift hamper market and in the end, I ditched the hamper company and continued to run the florists for the next three years until I sold the business.

Life has a way of moving us on!

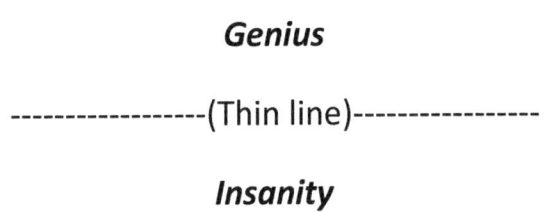

Genius

------------------(Thin line)-----------------

Insanity

CONCLUSION

It's all an illusion – so have fun with it!

This little book is designed to make you think. It's been written from the heart, telling inspirational stories of business owners who have been supported to play 'a bigger game' and so can you.

These business owners have looked adversity squarely in the eye and said 'screw you'.

I love people like that – because they're the seemingly 'crazy' ones that step up and are willing to step out. And in business and life, that's an amazing ability to have.

I hope that I've demonstrated through the stories, examples and the 'crazy business tips' that you too, are more than capable of joining the 'crazy gang', if you so choose.

Yes, my style is unconventional and it needs to be.

I shake things up a bit. I speak as I find (I really do try to put it nicely, but I believe in honesty in business, because it saves a lot of time, energy and money!).

I have a huge passion for helping business owners to succeed and to realise their dreams.

Anyone who can make a positive difference to the lives of others is an inspiration to me and therefore, in turn, I will physically (ok, metaphorically) move mountains and use all my business, marketing and personal expertise, knowledge and support to help them achieve their goals.

I even use the 'dirty word' HOLISTIC in the business arena and I'm proud to do so, because I work with business owners at every level – soulfully and strategically.

So, from one *crazy gang member* to another ... TTFN.

And thank you, because there is a reason you've just read this little book - right place, right time remember.

Love.

ABOUT THE AUTHOR

Heather Gifford is a very experienced business, product and service creator specializing in the SME sector.

She dedicates her time to helping people worldwide to set up businesses (positioning or re-positioning), assisting with new product development, packaging and UK/global promotion.

Over nearly two decades she has created, run and sold numerous companies of her own, in the service, manufacturing, retail and online sectors.   She is in an author, mentor and international business trainer.

Heather is also qualified in a range of mind, body and energy techniques that support business professionals to 'breakthrough' limiting beliefs and behaviors that may have restricted personal and professional growth.

Her home is in Wales, UK, with her two children. She is very grateful to be able to travel the world, getting paid for helping others to lead 'bigger and better' lives.

www.heathergifford.com

www.ingramcontent.com/pod-product-compliance
Lightning Source LLC
Chambersburg PA
CBHW071552170526
45166CB00004B/1643